V is for Victory

pamela fields

S.H.E. PUBLISHING, LLC

'V' is for Victory | Volume 5

Copyright © 2023 by Pamela Fields.

For information contact :

info@shepublishingllc.com

www.shepublishingllc.com

Book Cover and Title Page design by Michelle Phillips of

CHELLD3 3D VISUALIZATION AND DESIGN

ISBN :

978-1-953163-76-9 (paperback)

First Edition : February 2023

10 9 8 7 6 5 4 3 2 1

CONTENTS

V is for Victory

pamela fields

1 | GREATER RELEASE

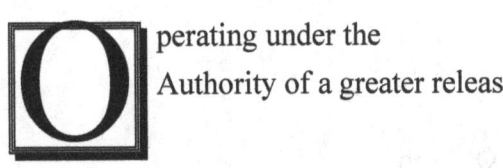

O perating under the
Authority of a greater release

A power of free will
    To the highest level

Looking back on a day when I was bounded
  With much sin, great fear

Perverse and evil spirits
  Sickness, injury and disease

A day when I found joy in the wicked deeds
  Of this world

The consumption of alcohol,
  Smoking and getting high,

    Caught up in a merry-go-round romance
    Going no where

Then the day came when I sought to be free

And found great joy, victory in all my endeavors

A deeper and profound love

For myself and those around me

A greater release

And now I choose thee O' Lord

Even though they fight me to no end

I choose thee.

2 | I SPELL YOUR NAME, JESUS

In my sleep as a Comforter

For my weary bones

On my sick bed, I spell thy name

As a Healer of all aliments.

When I'm broke and have no money

I spell your name as one who provides all my needs.

When I am hungry

Your name is Bread to my soul.

When I am weak

   I spell your name Strength.

Your name, I spell in the

   Midnight of life, Helper.

When I am heavy with the cares of this world,

   I spell your name as a Mighty Counselor.

When I am lonely, I spell your name

   As the Company Keeper which need no invitation.

In the darkest day

   L-i-g-h-t.

And when storm clouds are

   All around me, P-e-a-c-e.

O' mender of my heart,

When I am heart broken

I spell thee L-o-v-e.

3 | A PRESENT DAY FIGHT

When confronted with present
    Day challenges

Causing you to search your past
    Trying to correct those things

That you know you've wronged
    If only with an apology

And when you know nothing
    Within your strength can fix it

A simple acknowledgement
    Is all you can do

When searching your past
    Trying to find the root of the matter

What did I do to deserve this
    Your guiding thought

Realize this one thing is true…
    That the answer is not in the past

But rather in the present
    With odds on the hope

That you fall down and die
>Drop out of the race of humanity

Or simply change your mind
>On being a child of God

This my child
>Is a present-day fight

The only thing about your past
>That could affect a present-day fight

Is to understand that you
>Have an adversary

And that your adversary
>Have studied your past too

And knows your weaknesses
>But if you are a child of God

Nothing in your past can
>Bring about your doom

And your present-day fight
>Will be tomorrow's victory

4 | YOU'RE WELCOME

Let your flesh feast on the
Beauty of holiness
And let it rejoice and be
Exceedingly glad in it.

Let your spirit yield to
The spirit giver and
Dine on its words
That it might be strong,
Strengthen, prosper and grow.

Let your soul be blessed by
His majesty and His heavenly host
With a little heaven right here on Earth
A little peace and righteousness.

And may you yield your temple
In this place
And govern it in unity
With all the other temples here today.

For you are welcome,
You are welcome.

5 | THE BIG SECRET

With the coming of spring
Comes the quietest secret.

I look for it
Everywhere I go.

In the trees,
I look for it.

In the budding of a flower
In the greening of a single blade of grass.

The dawn of life
Is in the atmosphere.

The Earth wakes
And the stages of life
Presents its grand scene.

And when the big secret is unveiled,
The Earth is green again flowing with colors.

Of flowers blooming
In the midst of a spring shower.

6 | WHEN HURT, HURTS

When the tears of someone else's
    Pain reaches out and grabs.

When trouble strikes a loved one
    And triggers an emotion.

When poverty is accompanied
    With hunger,

Swells the belly
    And nakedness.

Eyes big and round
    Search for an answer,

Shaking the compassion
    Of others with force.

When disease multiplies
    Spreading with it,

An awesome and terrible
    Threat of doom.

Which pinches the core nerves
    Of pain that it hurts.

When hurt, hurts
    It's the beginning,

Of a riveting experience
    A hurt which touches others
        But you first.

7 | UNSPOKEN DIALOGUE

Words that will never be spoken
    Are not the easiest to digest

When understanding flows deeper than words
    Then you understand that saying them won't
        make a difference

So many unspoken words, an act of humility
    When incidents pile up covering up some

Of the good that is in your heart
    But self-control puts you in check

These piled up incidents puts you
    At the core of a pile of mess

Or it causes you to
    Redirect your focus

Unspoken words are recycled into prayers
    The more you hold in the more passionate the prayer

When there are times when you want to scream
    And all that is released are tears

Things a person has done
    Yet instead, you redirect your focus into prayers

Your fury brings you to a place of refuse
    A place where you can empty out and bury

Them in such a way that
    They'll never resurface

Words which are lashed out in hurt
    Cut and wound the spirit

Harsh and vicious words
    Do nothing to heal an already damaged soul

But to bring justice to these situations
    Have a little unspoken dialogue with Jesus
        who reads every one of your tears

8 | THE ROAD TO RECOVERY

After four days of school
    The spring vacation

Every hour of sound counsel
    And being in the right company

On a mission to find my son
    Going back over and over to a point
    Where he crossed the road

Putting on the fruits of understanding
    And clothed with patience, gentleness, and kindness

All this and the armor to stand
    Christ willed me this victory

No longer will I look back
    Pressing toward the road of recovery

Left, left, left, right, left
    Marching in God's army
    It's got to be right

The fight to recovery
    Seen in the small things that he do

His mind tells him to say 'no'
>But the soundness of his mind
>Puts him in check, and he does it anyway

An apologizing spirit
>And a growing interest in church
>And the word of God

Eating good food, no more smoking
>Feeding the mind a better menu

Staying away from those foul Rap Artist
>When that's cleared, perhaps those foul words
>Won't keep slipping

Plenty of love, flesh air
>And water

The road to recovery
>Will be a victorious path

One step at a time,
>A journey in the right direction

And when the battles come
>And the crossroads causes confusion

The pain is bearable
>With so many along the way to help

I'm closing the gate to the past
>On this road to recovery

I'm pressing on to victory
>Got some dreams to conquer
>Got some dreams to build

Got some growing to do
    This seed's planted deep
    And it's watered with his mother's tears

Thesé dreams I think I'll keep
    Got a few more years before I stretch out and die
    Got a few more years before I stretch out and die

9 | CAN'T STOP JESUS

Couldn't stop Him
When Pharaoh tried to
Kill the baby Moses

Couldn't stop Him
When He delivered
The people out of Egypt

Couldn't stop His birth
And couldn't stop His dying

And because He died
Can't stop me

My victory is established
My children
My healing
My finances
My ministry
Can't stop the Jesus in me either.

10 | FOLLOW
THE LEADER

Learned how to make my own footprints
Got my own footprints to make in this world

And I've learned how to enjoy my own company
Cause I know that along the way, each moment's shared

Don't have to cry no more
Through it all, I've pushed to a new level

The joy of the Lord makes me strong
His company to keep, His word to share

He's the leader that I follow
In faith do I press on toward the upper way

Don't wake me when I'm sleep
Sweet dreams and peaceful rest
Don't wake me when I'm sleep

Till morning comes sweet Jesus
Wake me unto a brand-new day

New mercies, I'll follow thee
O' Lord, till the day's end

My children are like the children of Isreal
      They are hardheaded, stiff-necked, rebellious
         And they follow after other people.

But they are my children, and I know their heart
      They shall never know my intention for them
         Until they learn who they are.

They shall never know my wealth
      Until they learn that they have within
         Themselves to make wealth come to them.

They shall never know peace
      Until they learn my God

They shall know no need
      But because they have a heart for people
         Their peace shall be greatly disturbed.

And they shall know my love
      And not be deprived of it

And so, they shall run to
      The House of Peace
         In each of their separate seasons

And like a work of art
     Your prayer will be accomplished

So, enjoy my gift unto you even now

Don't wait til the battle's
    Over, shout now

Your joy is complete
    This day, Amen, it is so.

12 | A WARRIOR'S PRIVATE WAR...

Caught in the middle of a struggle

A past which speaks out from the grave
Who suffered, bled and died
Many yet in bondage

Fighting to be freed
To see my family freed
To see my people freed

Then freed at last
Thank God Almighty
We're free at last

As a people,
To stand up and be counted
To exercise the rights, the same as all human race

But what has caused my people to wonder
In the wilderness, a vicious circle of failure
When so much need to be gained

No physical law to stop
Yet another kind of bondage do hinder

A fight is about to happen
A war of all wars

Caught in the middle of a struggle
    When the pressure of what's to come
        Is greater than what's past

When you been labeled a warrior
    There has to be a reputation
        Of a good fight

Cause a war isn't a war
    Unless you fight back

You've had to win a few
    Some great accomplishments worth mentioning

Yet how can you fight a war
    You can't see

But the evidence of what's happening
    Is marked on your people for all to see
        They've been whipped, repeatedly whipped

But right before the fight
    There comes great training

A time to observe the opponent
    A time to count the odds and to weight the balances

You've made up your mind
    Even before you really know

If I parish, let me perish
    And in the interim, it's evident
        That the giant must fall

Not by my will
    Nor my might
        But by God's spirit

13 | WHEN NEGATIVITY IS DEACTIVATED

The world is filled with negativity
Negativity tries to enter your world

It spills on you
It splashes on you

It's contaminated
And it's potent

I had a negativity attack today
What really makes these attacks
So hard to deal with is the mere fact
That you know the right thing to do

When you're overtaken by negativity
Reflex engines start up like a motor in a car

Being reminded of the power

To not only know the right thing to do

But the power to do the right things

Discharges all the engines and bring them to a halt

And the energy which was built up

To take action suddenly relaxes

I don't know which was worst

Reacting with reflexes and then being deactivated

Or just the mere thought that

I should have been on a level

Where the reflexes were not

Activated in the first place.

14 | WEARY OF WANTING

I grow weary of wanting

Wanting to be understood

Wanting to be heard

Wanting to be loved

Wanting to be warm

I grow weary of wanting

If I could see the reflection
Of my love toward you

If I knew the motivation of
Your kindness toward me

Are you motivated by the purity
Of your heart?

Or is there something else
Behind the motivation?

I grow weary of wanting

Wanting to see the reflection
Of my love toward you

Wanting to be cuddled in my lonely estate

Wanting my prosperity to flourish

Wanting the world to be at peace

I grow weary, so weary

My eyes ache with pain at the
Harshness and cruelty of the absence of love

Burning like a freezing fire
Is the world around me

Numbed by the cold
cold love

Never knowing the pain because
Of the numbness that freezes up like a wall

15 | A BITTER SPRING DAY

After a long, cold and bitter winter

Spring is waking up to the bitterness of war.

Splattered blood and tears of pain

The heavens cry out for peace.

16 | WHO'S ON BOARD?

After taking off on the plane of life

Many may come along to help you steer

But you land on your own

Now ask yourself, who's on board?

The answer is according to

Where you've landed in life

And if the plane has become

A wreck, a crash or afloat.

17 | WAKE UP SPRINGTIME

Springtime, wake up to me

You've slept through the cold winter

Now wake up
Through the budding of the green trees
And flowers that make up your gardens

Wake up to the cold world
And bring with it your warmth

Let your inner beauty
Locked up through harsh winter's wind
Release

In the gloomiest skies
Unleash a hint of purity

Let the echo of winter's dreary
Make room for a fresh breeze

Revisit us again Springtime

O' Springtime, shake the sleep from your eyes

Open up and see a starving world

Praise the heavens in the truth of thy beauty

Cry out for us
A world void of truth
Abstinent of brotherhood

Cry out for us
Your praise to heaven
And bloom again

Cry out your praise
In a bird's song

Let the cats and the dogs
Walk the streets together
If we who are brothers can't

I pray for my neighbors first
As they make their way
Through all of their woes

I pray that they find their way
And then I pray for this world
I pray for my family, in this order

O' Springtime
WAKE UP!!!

If this is not possible,
Then help me to find some warmth

Though I drink a cup of
Cold, cold world daily.

18 | MOMENTS BEFORE NIGHT TIME

I was just sitting here,
basting in the beauty of God's green earth

I've counted over 100 birds
currying here and there in bird's life

The breeze soothing and inviting

Nightfall is eagerly awaiting to conquer the day.

In the distant, birds tweeting everywhere

Cars zooming past in either direction

And children scream in active play

But if I wanted, I could tune it all out

I could if I wanted, slip right into a state of conscience
unconsciousness

If I allow my mind to focus on the
peacefulness of the moment

I could sit here forever and bath in this wonderful moment

A consciousness of the absence of stress and
its counterpart confusion

Night time has all but invaded the day

There's moments of a dim lit evening yet to go
before night time totally set in

Street lights are already lit

The sounds of night time are absent
of the chirping birds and cries of children

And right now, only a barking dog
can be heard in the distance

Opening up to a communication
of other dogs barking in the near distance

And the cars zooming in either direction

Night time has creeped in.

19 | A LOVE LETTER

Who, pure and true, is my lover?
Upon my pillow, in sweet dreams I ponder

No words can effectively describe

Love of tenderness so sweet
Love of kindness so pure

No, words can't effectively describe

Love of happy communication
Love that takes the heart beat

Let the world see, let them recognize

Let them see it in the way
The morning breaks through the darkness of
Twilight

Let them see it in the way
The seasons change and flatters the heart
With its distinctive beauty

It's in the way that the birds chirp
And the squirrels chatter,
The dogs' bark and cats' meow
Which help me reflect on my inner beauty

That your joy ignites my joy
And our peace, forever symbolic of our love

Let the honey, sweet as it is
But let your words to me be forever sweeter

And let the evidence of our love be seen in our giving
For in our togetherness are we complete

Oh! When the storms come
Take me in your arms and comfort me in your asurety,
For we are one

In troubled waters and in the thickest forest,
Lead me to the safest shore,
To the piercing light that leadeth,
For you are my hero

I've set my hopes and affection on a sure thing
The only one to love me is Thee
And Thee, only do I love

No father or mother
    Nor brother or sister
            Not son or daughter
                    Not even spouse, or friend
                            Has moved me like Thee

But rather, your love
Has called me to an even deeper and greater love for them

A growing concern, busting on the inside of my soul
A pressing matter,
every venture brings me closer with Thee

Speak to me my love;
Let your words echo within my thirsty soul

Speak to me my love;
Let your words sing as the birds sing each morning

Let the budding of spring,
The sprinkle of morning's due speak true words of love to me
And when the sun comes,
Let me bass in its beauty because you created it

Speak to me my love;
Let your words chase my fears away
Speak to me my love;
Let your words command my role today

The way that I should walk
The way I should talk
How to wear my hair
What dress to wear

Speak to me my love when loneliness creep upon me
And the busyness of the day is past
Speak to me at last, my love

I'm like Mary and Martha
I am thou humble servant,
I'm going to work for you
But forsake me not a time to worship
And to minister at your feet, I pray

20 | PURPOSE OF STRUGGLE

I struggle through life
On purpose

That purpose grips my survival
And takes me where I want to go

Right back to a struggle of the fragile soul
Of a people precious and destitute for time

A want, a need, a hunger
Against a ticking end

Where time is not an ally
And my purpose is still a struggle

21 | PRAY FOR ME, PRAY FOR ME

If by chance you see me walking
    With my head bowed down

If perhaps I do not greet you
    With an outstretched hand

If my countenance be always shadowed
    By a frown

Don't be angry
    Just pray for me, pray for me.

May be tired, may be weary
    May be wounded deep within

If I stop and rest a while
    This journey once more to begin

When O' younder, streets of gold
    And a heaven I shall stand

You'll be happy
    Just pray for me, pray for me.

22 | DAMAGED, BRUISED AND SCARRED

Damaged, bruised and scarred for life,
Like spoiled meat, damaged and only to be disposed.

Rotten in the belly of this earth,
Making me sick enough to vomit.

Damaged goods that malfunction,
When left in a dysfunctional society.

Bruised and sorely discarded flesh,
Tender with limited opportunity to heal.

Scarred with the memory of the hurt,
Only physically mended, but mental flashbacks still ache.

Damaged, bruised and scarred,
Little children of the world.

Who can see beyond the eyes,
And see into the soul?

Who can know beyond the outward physical fitness
The heart and mind of the matter?

Who can answer the rattling questions
Beginning with why?

Why so much bitterness?
Why so much hate and unforgiveness?
Why so much sin?

Damaged, bruised and scarred by the actions of other people,
Plucked from life and thrown in a barrel of rotten apples.

23 | PEACE BE STILL

The whole world is a storm,
  Incontrollable, boisterous and tempest.

To many the sounds of thunder behind thunder,
  The clash of lighting and the threat of flood
      May not be threatening.

Others may seemingly not even notice
    That their future is affected by the
        outcome of this storm.

I am reminded of our Lord, Jesus
    As He laid asleep amid a storm at sea,
        Merely spoke the words, Peace be still.

And while we're all affected by
    these uncertain outcome,
          Prayer is the only ship that Jesus is on
              It is unsinkable and quite sturdy.

And when riding in the ship of prayer,
    Jesus, carest thou not that I perish?

When the raging storms are all around,
    Preparest thou me a ship of prayer to sail upon.

And when that ship begins to rock,
 and threatens to sink.

Send thy word out to fight for me,
 "Peace and be still."

24 | THE CHARACTERS OF MY PRAYERS

The characters of my prayers don't like me.

Their spirits are being held captive by demon spirits;

That mean them no good and would like to destroy me.

And since these spirits are domineering their life,

Controlling their decisions, thoughts, and attitudes

Thereby creating a tool to fight against

The spirit of Christ which lives in my life.

Like a basketball game,

The characters of my prayers

Opponents and keeping score.

My members and all of me

Are the star players because Jesus is on board.

I've got my focus in view, and everyday

The characters of my prayers are in

Opposition against me and everyday we play

One against the other trying to win,

Having complete control to the ball
But one day, the play offs.

The characters of my prayers is on the opposite team.
I play back with kindness, patience,
love and peace strengthen with joy.
They are good players and I must have them on my team.
I must somehow unite us.
They are my family, my neighbors, friends, and fellow brothers.

They are people that I love and have grown to love.
They are fighting for the wrong team
And they don't know it.

With all that is in me
I know that greater is He that's in me
Than that which is in them. (1John 4:4)
Though their members strong,
One shall chase a thousand
And two shall chase ten thousand. (Deut. 32:30)
My weapon not carnal, but mighty
Through prayer to the pulling down of strongholds. (2 Cor. 10:4)
These kind come out only through fasting and prayer.

And so the spirit of witchcraft warring against their mind,
The spirit of addiction, the spirit of lust,

Must submit to that greater authority in me.
Strongholds of schizophrenia which
control and posses must be cast out.
The characters of my prayers are dirty with sin.
They are ugly from the reflection of evil which holds them bondage.
They are sick with the affliction of disease which cripples them.
And so, to these spirits and to the spirit of suicide and murder
am I preparing for the play offs.
They will be free; the battle is already won.

25 | IT'S A MESS IN THIS PLACE

What comprises the inside of a man are the things we cannot see.
Where I come from, the inward side of a man is what we see.
Not his physical beauty, the spirit of a man.
And my spiritual eyes can see that there's a mess in this place,

The Earth:
I took a long journey and ended up in a place called Earth.
My home is far away from here and one thing is sure, I can't go back
the way I came.

What Do I Do:
Do I turn my head in disgust, pretending that I don't see the mess?
Do I choke up and laugh, or add to the clutter by doing the things they do?
Or do I clean this litter up one piece at a time?

The Decision:
Setting an example for others to follow by keeping clean my spirit
Washing out the stains of sin and keeping it clean with the Word of God
Keeping the body of Christ uncluttered until we all operate in the
same likeness of mind.

'V' IS FOR VICTORY
v es para la victoria
INTERMISSION

26 | A CURE, DELIVERANCE

The responsibility of the saints of God today
Those that are called mine,

Make my house peaceful
Let it be a safe haven

Cause the storm is coming
The place whereby

The people can run in
For shelter, safety and serenity

The storm is here to stay
There is peace in my shelter

Those that come into my shelter
Will find peace

Where there is peace
The foundation for deliverance
There you will find the cure

The good care of my people
Will foster the right environment for healing

I will wash my people with peace
And the rinse cycle is where they will find deliverance
Peace is the beginning of healing

There is a noisome pest
Which has invested my people with the disease of sin

Our mission is to kill the germ
Don't let the germ live, find a resting place in your heart
Seek peace in the house that is called mine.

27 | EVERY MOVE COUNTS

Careful study of where you are in life,
Close evaluation of where you want to be
Practical use of valuable time,
Because EVERY MOVE COUNTS.

Constant planning,
Trying to defeat all the obstacles,
Checking up on progress,
Because EVERY MOVE COUNTS.

Like a game of chess,
The enemy's in constant view,
Then up from behind, Checkmate,
I told you, EVERY MOVE COUNTS.

Out of weakness, one slip,
No time to lose, pressure is on every side,
Gaining the upper edge, do something quick,
Because EVERY MOVE COUNTS.

Lightning and thunder, terrible rainfalls
Lest I make my move hasty
I could get caught, soak, wet, drench,
Because EVERY MOVE COUNTS.

Infancy, terrible two's, toddler, preschool,
Timetables, sweet sixteen, two years to go,
Driver's education, graduation, college tuition,
No time to lose, because EVERY MOVE COUNTS.

Lazy days are all gone past.
School's out, school's in, lazy days and all that jazz,
Be creative days, be smart days, caught up days,
Because EVERY MOVE COUNTS.

28 | THAT KIND SPIRIT

that kind spirit shines

that kind spirit draws

that kind spirit shares

that kind spirit forgives and forgets

that kind spirit cares

that kind spirit smiles

that kind spirit laughs

that kind spirit gives

that kind spirit loves

that kind spirit

is the kind of spirit
that you would recognize.

29 | FINDING THE EXIT IN A DESPERATE SITUATION

In a hot and burning building
As smoke raises to the top
And smothering smoke, thick masses
Preventing me from clearly seeing
The path that I should go
As it seeks to snuff out
The life running freely
And flowing through my veins

Quickly a door, a window
I must find an exit
To safety
But it's hard to see the way
Please somebody
Anybody please
Show me the way.

Finding an exit in a desperate situation.

Across the short span of life
In a world of:
Positives and negatives
Ups and downs
Ins and outs
Crazy turn arounds
There comes a time
When we'll find ourselves
Down and out
In a negative situation.

Trying to find the exit in a desperate situation.

Desperate situations of
Pain and grief
Affliction and addiction
Hopelessness and bondage
Guilt and shame
Stupor and ignorance
Oppression and depression

Desperate situations, obstacles which hide the exit.

30 | MIRACLES

Miracles of today are
    Much different from the
        Miracles of yesterday.

We need to look a little closer,
    There are miracles of all sorts
        All around us and even now.

We have doctors today
    And big fine hospitals
        Where once there were none.

Universities to prepare
    A man in the study of
        Medicine and healing.

When Jesus reigned on Earth
    This was not the case
        And so many people suffered.

Until the miracles of Jesus
    Healed their ailing bodies
        And they were set free.

Yesterday, the miracles of God
     Were seen through His healings
          And talked about throughout the land.

Where today it's a miracle
     To walk out of one's own
          House and to return safely.

The miracles of God are seen
     Everywhere, even the choices
          That some people make in life.

To have the baby rather than abort
     The decision not to start smoking
          And the choice to stay in school.

31 | LIGHTS, CAMERAS, ACTION

This scene takes place on the south side of town
In a moderately income neighborhood
Where there is one corner in particular
In which God zooms His lenses into focus.

Under the spotlights of heaven
A group of young men rehearse
As they approach the stage
Their individual parts in this simple act.

As they carry out the script
Marketing their wares
Up until the wee hours of
The morning's dawn.

I've got your good times right here
Nickel bags, dime bags, rocks and sticks
The hand of God is not pleased.

Building your future on a curse
You should be laying up prayers
During the scenes of your life.

This world was built on prayers you know
We did not get this far by ourselves
Our ancestors, grandmothers
And great grands prayed and prayed.

Many never asking anything for themselves
Just to see their children free
Abraham's obedience to God
Paved the way for his seeds to be blessed.

And now that you are free
Your performance
Your all-night dance
As you serve in the streets.

The angels of the night are watching you
The trees, the birds, the squirrels
And every creeping thing sees you
They breathe your wicked seeds of evil deeds.

The seed is released into the universe
And comes back as a strike against you
The cameras are rolling
It's your life, you can't deny.

The Bible says,
"Every seed reproduces after its kind"

Those righteous deeds will come back in righteous seeds
Likewise, your deeds of wickedness.

The people of this neighborhood
Both young and old
Have seen your previews
And have read your reviews.

They know why you're there
We all are aware of your activities during the night
You are the main character in the scenes of your life
And on the day of judgment, the cameras will roll.

32 | A MOTHER CRIED

 oke up one morning
   Mind heavy and torn

 epressed and troubled
   In spirit

 ocused on the problem
   Weak with depression

 mother cried.

33 | NUMB, FROM THE NECK DOWN

I'm numb from the neck down,
To what my eyes have seen
And what my ears have heard

Heresies with evil intent
Backbiting and malicious gossip
From those of your own household

Scripture talks of this type of enemy
It's a sign of the day in which we're living in

Lips, lying lips that whisper sweetly, "I love you,"
Are the same that tear and pull at the tentacles of my heart

A mind that play by the rules while it's day
But at the first the sun fades, games well-hidden with no rules

Hands that give where it's not needed
Only to boast, "I gave."
Are the same hands that take more than a share

Who can love such an unrighteous heart?
None but the pure in heart,
None but the pure in heart.

And through a bruised heart
And much lack

Through tear-stained eyes
And sobs of grief

Burst forth joy that overwhelms
And smother out the stigma and scars
That show the pain of this world

Please, please
Smother my heart with joy

The joy of the Lord
Numbs my body from the neck down
To the pains of this world

34 | SINFUL TOOLS

People of the world
Bank on the fact
That much of what they do
Is concealed by materials of matter

The thoughts that they think
Is concealed where no
Other can know

Hiding much of what they
Do behind house of clay
Where no other can see

But what if this matter
Became a screen of smoke
Which fades away to reveal all

And houses of glass
Where all can see
The wicked seeds and tools of sin

What would they do if like
Adam and Eve, in the Garden
They became naked and all their sin revealed

If the sinful tools that they use
Reflected somehow that all
Would know

What if the demons which invest
Themselves in the hearts of people
Spoke out with its own mine
Or showed up like a mole

What if the hand that went into your purse
And stole your money spoke out and said
In an incontrollable voice, "I did it, I took the money."
Or if the fingers just fell off and somehow
All would know the reason

And those who lie before a court of law
Are exposed for the murder they did commit
As they try to hide behind the matter of secret thoughts

Or the homosexual who try
To hide behind the clothes
Of his sex

Or the voice which says with anticipation,
"I love you," And his cheating heart exposed
Unpredictable and without warning

But of great importance, the crimes
Which people commit in secret against little children
Will never be able to do it again because the
Nakedness of their crime will be exposed before all people

35 | GOD'S MAN

In this large city of
  Modern day architecture

Cathedrals and temples
  And landscapes divine

A stranger came to town
  Found a great big pretty building

And said, "It's God's will that I work here."

Now the church building was
  Only open but a couple of days

And as he read the bulletin
  The church service posted

In a beautiful glass column
  It read, next service, Sunday morning.

So the stranger came to the
Sunday morning service

He asked to speak to the Overseer,
The Pastor, Assistant, Ministers, and Deacons

He introduced himself as
Merely God's man

Many attended the service that morning
But when the blind man walked in
He knew why it had to be this church

The opening prayer went forth and
The scripture was read

Man's program started at 11:00 a.m.
But God's program was about to intervene

At 11:55 the Holy Ghost fell
Man's program and all flesh could not keep up
The blind man received his sight
And many were healed. When the spirit of God
Lifted, many were still drunk in the spirit.

The testimonies went out
Through the surrounding neighborhoods

The Overseer, Pastor, Assistant, Ministers and Deacons
　　Met and declared that it's revival time.

Each night of the revival the crowds began to swell
　　More and more attended
And as large as the church was,
　　There was standing room only

Then there came a night where the church building
　　Could not hold any more people, standing or otherwise
The people piled in droves on the street
　　And the press was great

The news of God's man had traveled through the city
　　It whispered of a stranger in the city that's healing
And the reports and testimonies also traveled
　　To the neighboring cities

And just outside the outskirts of the city
　　Laid a great man of God
One who had dedicated countless hours in prayer for others
And devoted the life which God gave to him in the service of God

He laid there in great pain
　　Desirous of death

And he wondered with much doubt in his weakened and delirious
    Estate, "Is anybody praying for me?"

That night the calls were made among a few of his dearest friends
    It was decided that they would take him to see this stranger

"Who's going to pay for this damage?"
    The Overseer, Pastor, Assistant, Ministers and Deacons
Looking up at the great hole in the ceiling used to lower the man
    As he laid in great pain on his bed
Lowered by some men and a rope.

God's man simply replied
    Where have you heard of in this day
That people are breaking into the church service

These are days where God would have to anoint
    Men and women with special gifts to keep
The devil's devices out of the church
    And to convert those that are bound
This is not my doing, but God's.

36 | THERE IS A JONAH IN MY SHIP

When storms come
And you've considered all the things
surrounding your situation

You're doing all you can to serve God
You're living saved all you know how

You're fasting
You're praying and reading your Bible

And the storms still won't cease
You're ready to move forward

But the struggle prevents the prevail
Your purpose is pure

Your intentions noble
Crossing every 't' and dotting every 'I'

You're clear about it not being for selfish gain
But the increase still won't come

When you've named it
Claimed it, confessed with your mouth
About that which concerns you

And know that there is no real reason
Why you shouldn't or can't cross over the barrier

Then it's time to realize
You've got a Jonah on your ship

But you can't realize you got a Jonah on the ship
Until you get to the point that you're willing to do
something about it

Storms come and storms go
But this storm came and never really left

When you're dodging thunder like bullets
And lightnings like arrows

The steps of a good man are ordered by the Lord
And every step you make God has to send somebody
To pull you up out of the snares

But when you face your Jonah dead in the eyes
And say within your heart that you're breaking through this barrier

Then the vision can be fulfilled
Your blessings are on the other side of the barrier

Manifold blessings held back
By the devil himself,
enough to try every measure of your salvation

Now the window is not dirty anymore
The vision is no longer stained, the focus is clear

Bullseye, I've found
What I was aiming for.

37 | GREATER WORKS

It really doesn't matter
    That others see my light shinning
        But that it shines.

It doesn't matter that others observe my prayer
    But it does matter that I pray.

It doesn't matter that I tell you I have faith
    But it does matter that faith is displayed.

It really doesn't matter that my riches show
    But that I am rich.

It really doesn't matter that I sing before men
    But that my heart sings.

It doesn't matter what others do or say,
    But it does matter what I do or say.

Lord, if no one else sees my good
    I pray that you see.

What appears to be prosperous is empty.
    What appears to be empty is prosperous.

And when I work, it doesn't matter who sees,
    But it does matter that I work.

For if I work Jesus, the product, the evidence,
    And the reflection of my labor will spark.
        And the glow from it will shine back to the top.

38 | THE OTHER SIDE OF FREEDOM

Days upon days

Always more days

Seeking for the other side

Of the next day

A world enclosed

Inside another world

Where screams and tears

Are locked away unheard and hidden

Chains, cells and keys

Chains that jingle

Cells of steel

And keys that lock

The other side of freedom is prison

Prison locks you away from your dreams and goals

And separates loved ones and past acquaintance

Prison whether physical or mental

Whether chains are visible or invisible

Real just the same when it stripes from you
The simplest of human choices
And takes away your right to make decisions

The freedom of choice
No other animal possess
Man, made in the image of God
Given the divine power of command

And demands his choices
With the simple words of 'yes' and 'no'

When at last I break free
From these chains
Never again will I look at time
But rather, every step that lead to my goals in life

39 | AFTERMATH

The aftermath of dealing with something disastrous in your life
Is dealing with your mind in trying to figure out why.

The why it all happened
The how it could have been avoided

And the what it's going to take
To clean it up

The aftermath of situations

And circumstances that come about

The aftermath of eviction

The aftermath of a separation between loved ones

The aftermath of incarceration

The aftermath of divorce

The aftermath of unfavorable court orders

Learning to live with

The aftermath of a sunken vessel

The aftermath of losing a valuable job

The aftermath of sickness of a love one

The aftermath of sickness of self

The aftermath of death of a loved one

The aftermath, a very dry and thirsty place
Nothing can really quench

A door toward bitterness and sorrow
Only keep your mind focus on a well of everlasting water

The aftermath of a burdensome and heavy load
No one can really carry such a load alone

Give it over to the Lord Jesus
He'll make your burdens light

The aftermath, your cross to bear
A thorn in the flesh

A valley in the shadow of death
God will make a way

The aftermath, a dark and dusty road
Christ is the answer, He's the light that shines bright

He'll give you rest
He'll give you peace
He'll give you joy

The aftermath, a lost and lonely way
A 12:01 situation, a dreaded time
That time which you feared, come upon you
Seek Him, and you will find an answer.

40 | BITE SIZE PIECES

We all are babes in God's sight

Some of us may be still on milk
But others are struggling with the meat

Bite size pieces

With each promotion that we get
While we're yet soldiers in training

Each round is just as hard as the first
Bite size pieces

Each test comes with its own set of instructions
Yet with each, one rule remains the same, preparation

The essential key which unlocks every door
Bite size pieces

Making ready for the day
When all you have to give

Puts you in the negative
>Whether emotionally, financially or physically so

No one sees nor understands
>But everybody concludes that your deeds are not of God

When they observe your negative estate
>Not unlike Job's dear friends

Traveled from afar and without any words spoken
>Concluded that his deeds to be devious

Bite size pieces

The only witness that can see
>Is the only witness that can not speak

The left hand observes
>When others can only falsely accuse

A steak prepared with no tenderizer
>Charcoal broiled, and well done
Bite into that dry piece of meat
>Bite size pieces

Job's friends were not eating the same
>Piece of meat that he was chewing on

They did not understand that
    The flavor was not seasoned for taste

Therefore, it doesn't matter
    Whether you like it or not

Whether you're hungry or not
    But to complete the test is to finish the steak

Cut into bite size pieces.

41 |

COMPOUNDED
FOCUS

A series of problems
> One behind the other
>> And sometimes doubling up

Trying to prevent
> The joy of the Lord
>> And the peace of God

It's when you're earmarked for trouble
> When you're in between blessings
>> And when there is a lack on every hand

A deep valley with the only way out is up
> A maze with unmarked exits like a forest
>> Or a vicious circle

Feeling your way in the dark
> Being pulled down by the weights of the world
>> A search for answers only to find none

Weary and worn
    Threads of hope,
        Keeps me going

Like crossing the street to another side
    The onset of busy traffic with no let up
        But the other side is in view

The other side, the hope, the ultimate focus
    But these compounded focus, problems
        Like busy traffic, won't seem to go away

Problems, things that get in our way
    And clog up our receptacle in seeing the ultimate focus
        Asking Jesus the question: Carest thou not that we
        perish? (Mark 4:37-38)

When your focus should be on Jesus, and you'll have joy
    Your focus should be on the Prince of Peace and you'll have peace
        Your focus should be on the Great I Am and you'll
        have the answers to all your problems

Compounded focus is a trick of the enemy
    It's a war in the mind which appear real
        It causes a struggle and occupies too much of
        your time and thought

The other side of struggle
    Won't happen until you
        Lay those burdens down

Speak to the mountain
    And be thou moved

Compounded focus,
    When you're in a deep valley

Speak to the mountain
    Then turn around and
        Speak to the other mountain

42 | THE SCIENCE OF THE CRUCIFIXION

One who died for our sins
    Crucified on the cross

His disciples saw Him
    His mother saw Him
Mary Magdelene who wiped His feet with her hair saw
    Him

The science of the crucifixion
    Was not the death of our Lord

No, it was not how He laid
    Down His life

It was not the way the Roman
    Soldiers arrested Him

As they took Him from Judgement Hall
    To Judgement Hall
Trying to find a charge
    Why they should persecute Him

The science of the crucifixion
    Was not in the custom of the Jewish people

How they would put
    Their criminals to death

It was not the nails
      Driven through our Lord's hands

It was not the tree that
      He hung on

It was not even the
      Piercing in His side

The science of the crucifixion
      Was not the death of our Lord

But that He rose again
      And lives

It is the foretelling of His
      Miraculous birth

It is that which was
      Prophesied through the generations

The science of the crucifixion
      Was not the death of our Lord

That was the love of God

The science is that He lives and
      Reigns and is an intercessor for us
At the right hand of the Father.

43 | SILENCE

Silence screams out
   a piercing alarm
      of dread and horror

In the face of the terrible odds
   our youth must go through and yet
      our silence screams out as we watch

Like a painted picture
   our expressions and attitudes
      have been seen by all

But the paint brush can't
   give us voice, and one's
      interpretation is his own

Like a vicious cycle
   The response from the
      Interpretation, silence

Its expression and its attitude
   are only a reflection of yours
      but where is the voice?

Who will voice the horrible truth?
     or who will speak up and regard the issues?
          are the only speech, trumped up lies?

Silence scream when our
     expression to drug traffic
          turns and look the other way

Silence scream when our
     attitude on worldly issues
          make us feel our opinions don't count

Silence scream out when
     drive by and gang violence
          plant the seed of fear in out heart

Silence scream at the
     alarming statistics of teen
          pregnancy and unwed mothers

Silence scream and we
     may have to repent cause the
          voices of ill will cries louder

Silence scream when we are not motivated by
     our expressions and our attitudes and they are
          puffed up clouds of smoke that fades in the air

Silent screams have allowed
     our innocent youth to be murdered
          like the soldiers at battle time

No one hears the missiles
    aim and shoot their targets
        no one hears the victims
            drop like ragged dolls
                as the supportive arms
                    of a little child let go

No one hears the silent screams
    smothered and muffled against
        the street lights and traffic of the big city

No one hears but
    the voice is the only one
        who can make a difference in silence

44 | SINNERS DIE YOUNG TOO

Oh, what a glorious day

> When we make our pilgrimage up heaven's way
>
> When we stand before the judgment seat
>
> And after the story is all told, we hear
>
> "Well done, thou good and faithful servant."

Oh, what a glorious day that will be.

But there is something mighty pathetic about a man

> Who stand before a righteous judge only to hear
>
> "Depart from me, your work is of iniquity."
>
> Sinners die young too you know.

It is sad to think that in hell, will they spend eternity.

It's sad because the same opportunity comes to all men.

> The word of God says, and I quote:
>
> "I would that no man would perish.
>
> But the fearful and unbelieving and
>
> The abominable, and murderer, and
>
> Whoremongers, and sorcerers and

Idolaters, and all liars shall have their

Part in the lake which burneth with

Fire and brimstone: which is the second death." (Rev. 21:8)

It is sad to think that the things of this world

Have blinded the minds of sinners

And they won't believe.

They won't invest in

The possibility and the hope

Of a better place when they die.

Most men understand the fact

That they must lie down in a cold grave one day.

That their body will decade back to dust and

Their eternal soul will no longer exist in this realm.

Only God can look into the spirit of a man and determine his destiny.

Beyond this life, one can only hope.

What lies ahead of today is anyone's guess.

So if someone walk up to you and say, "God is."

Who is to say that He isn't?

Because what is really sad, is that you might

Find out for yourself a lot sooner than you think.

One of the saddest things to ever witness

Is to see a man's body being lowered into the grave

And his life exemplified the life of a sinner

But it's sad because you know the promises of God

But to the sinner a lake of fire

When you think of the many opportunities he had

The same as you and me, today and each day we live.

Cause someone need to know that sinners die young too.

45 | A PART OF ME IS DYING

Let my presence be disguised
And my mission overtake me.

As the real passion of my heart ache,
A pain with every beat.

The joy of the Lord is my strength
Even in the face of so much pain.

A flow of tears unleashed on a situation
Which needs much mending.

Prayers of faith causes me to be strong
When I would normally not.

Let my mind not see
The destruction of your path.

Let me go away, hide and not see
The errors of your ways.

Words which see but won't speak
And bury themselves in utter shame and humility.

Words which speak but
Won't hear the plot and ultimate fall.

Words which chase and pursue
Words which wave in the air, yet still are not heard.

Words which speak through action and deeds
Are taken and never thought of again.

Let my presence be concealed and
My purpose spring forth.

Let faith perform for me
What my eyes see not.

A part of me is dying
When I have so much to give.

46 | AN EMERGENCY PRAYER

Somehow Father, the show must go on.
Come rain, snow, sleet or hail,
The curtains will come up.

And as we rehearse the script
To the most important scenes that govern our lives,
From where I stand, we don't quite seem ready.

Important roles in the rock of these ages.
Slip ups, and identity crisis
Demand failure.

The table is set Lord, but will the guest arrive?
The invitations sent and the programs printed.
A command performance, you must take center stage.

Everything, positively everything is ready, but the cast…?
I should be happy, but I'm truly not.
With all the roles that I must play, tis not an easy thing to do.

My script just doesn't seem to fit in with the rock of these ages.
Like time has taken a scene from the pages of the past,
And pasted it in the balances of an era with an uncertain ending.

Uncertain, because the happily ever after ending

Which I am accustomed are looking directly at a season
Of abuse, addiction, disobedience, and rebellion.

Father, command the roles of each character.
Speak the words, and let your words not return unto you void.
Let not the rocks cry out your praise, but command you a people.

As you promised and I quote, the role of the unsaved
Husband will be saved by the sanctified wife, and her household
Then let their roles be manifested this day.

What you've done for me, you can do it again I pray.
If the daughter comes against the mother
And the son against the father,

Then their roles contradict the ending for this scene
Because if the mother be a saved mother, then
This household shall be saved this day, again I pray.

Please Sir, having the testimony
Of being a saved mother for more than ten years
Of this life which you have given me.

Being fire baptized and Holy Ghost filled,
I beseech your throne of mercy,
Stir up, shake and mold that which is already yours.

Please Sir, accept my down payment of faith
And that faith may be manifested,
Command this performance.
The stage is set and the curtains about to rise,
In an emergency such as this,
All I can do is pray.

47 | PRAYERS FROM THE HEART OF A BLACK WOMAN

Unselfish words uttered between me and Thee

Take its focus upon yet another fight.

Words take flight up upon a spiritual bird.

Take these words between me to Thee.

Mothers, raise your children from your knees in prayer.

Less a spiritual giant come upon you and yours.

Pray for words of wisdom, to instruct and to teach.

A feast of words to uplift and encourage.

Protect, Father, this day and let your will be done

Thank you and Amen.

48 | SWEET AND SURE

So many times I've beseeched
Your throne, Dear Lord

Prayers full of strength
And faith

And today, I refuse to cry
When I've yet haven't heard

Weary eyes that search and
An abundance of hope won't cease

Cause somehow there will
Come an answer sweet and sure.

Jesus, if the prayer that I pray
Be held up in forth coming

Then I pray that you
Bless some other soul

Bless them to be a
Blessing unto me, Amen.

Bless that other soul
To come by my house

Let them be the vehicle that you use to
Draw that sinner man and those hardheaded children.

Bless that other soul financially and let their
Blessing overflow enough to be a blessing unto me.

Let someone else see my
Struggles and intercede in my behalf.

For my house and my car and
For my miracle breakthrough.

Let that sickness be cursed and
Dried up when they lay hands on me.

And when I see the fate of my people
Their sinful state, let someone else see it too.
And have just a little
Talk with you about it.

Let the answer come sweet and sure,
But that it come is my prayer.

Let that other soul pray a prayer that it come
And let that other soul be blessed.

Amen

49 | WITHDRAWALS

You will know when you're addicted to drugs
    And any of life's habit-forming pitfalls.

The cost is far greater than the price you've paid
    To purchase these life-threatening perils.

But when the currency is exhausted, it's the withdrawals
    That lets you know you're addicted.

It comes with an early warning signal of cravings and
    Mere wishes to have something which seems
    Virtually impossible to acquire at the given time.

Perhaps you're trying to kick the habit
    But before you know it, the habit's kicking you.

Well, life has its withdrawals too. When you can't
    Continue to get those simple things in life
    For which you've become accustomed to.

Withdrawals are negative situations for which
    We find ourselves. A lack or a need situation.

We go to the bank, we make a withdrawal.

Depression can cause us to withdraw from society.
  A withdrawal in the spirit from a lack of spirituality.
    And a whole lot of other negative experiences.

But Lord, If thou withdraw thyself from me
  No other help I know.

God is really all that's needed to turn those negative
  Situations into positive ones.

He'll make your negative habits work for your good.
  Give you a testimony that He can.
    And cause you to use this positive report to help
    others.

What the devil meant to destroy you
  God will use to help you to build with.

50 | THE CHILL IS GONE

My lover has left town
And there is no sign of
Him any where.

And while I really don't
Know for sure that he's
Really gone

Cause he didn't say bye
I'll see you later
Or anything.

But I know he's gone away
Because my heart
Felt the breakup.

Winter fades into spring
Away with my sloppy sweaters
And floppy hats.

Away with the wool suits
And cozy big
Over coats, boots and mittens.

Or the fur coat that
Makes me feel so warm,
Secure and protected.

With spring closely at hand
I'll have to submit to its rules
And govern myself to that season.

Longer day light
Budding greenery
And much rain.

And then one day
I'll wake up
And it'll be gone.

The long hot summer and then
The autumn leaves
Will turn and begin to fall.

Then boldly my lover will return
Snow ball fights as it piles up.
As snow covers the limbs of trees.

Cold nights in front of a warm cozy fire
Let's me know that now
The chill is really gone.

ACKNOWLEDGMENTS

First and foremost, I'd like to thank God for allowing me to go through my journey of life in which I have been able to learn and grow from my circumstances and change my challenges into this beautiful work of art and book series of poems.

And to my mother, Leola Reynolds, who told the best stories when I was growing up. My love for her and her stories she told us as we were growing up were quite splendid.

And to my readers, I am grateful for your support. I'd like to offer some wisdom. When an older person has a story to tell, sit down and listen because it will be a good story, one of true wisdom.

ABOUT THE AUTHOR

Pamela Fields was born to Gentle Frank Fields and Leola Reynolds on the south side of Chicago, Illinois. Growing up in Chicago, she attended various elementary schools and Wendell Phillips High School. Pamela later pursued her education at Harold Washington Junior College, where she focused on Early Childhood Education. Recognizing the importance of ensuring no child is left behind and no older adult is left uncared for, she was driven to choose this major. Additionally, she attended Prestige Nurse Aide Training Academy, earning her certification as a CNA.

As the oldest among her siblings, which include one sister and two brothers, Pamela refers to them as "stair-steps" due to their one-year age differences. She credits her siblings and her mother's second husband, Richard Reynolds, as her role models who equipped her with valuable insights and strategies for navigating the world. Pamela is a loving mother to three children: Nikia Fields, Edward Fields, and Shana Edwards. Her children have brought her immense joy, and she cherishes her role as a grandmother to her eight grandchildren, providing them with educational materials through her homemade learning lessons.

Professionally, Pamela has held positions at various early learning centers. In addition, she worked as a CNA on weekends and dedicated her evenings to caring for her mother. Her diverse employment experiences ultimately led her to her desired destination—an inspiring author who aspires to become a best-selling writer through S.H.E. PUBLISHING LLC. Simultaneously, she embarked on starting two businesses: K.I.N.D.N.E.S.S. Kare (Keys IN Developing & Navigating Effective Social Solutions), a childcare service, and Pam's Baking Handz.

Pamela's ultimate purpose and passion revolve around uniting ordinary individuals, including herself and others, with a shared commitment to promoting love and compassion. She firmly believes that small efforts such as a friendly smile, expressions of gratitude, prayer, and acts of kindness can gradually transform the world—one day, one hour, and one second at a time. She emphasizes that a simple smile takes only a second, and kindness comes at no cost.

Thanks for reading!
Please add a short review on
Amazon and S.H.E. PUBLISHING LLC.
Let me know your thoughts!

www.ingramcontent.com/pod-product-compliance
Lightning Source LLC
Chambersburg PA
CBHW011216120626
46545CB00008B/3015